Tiger Talk
Get Into Science

Using Tools

Leon Read

SEA-TO-SEA
Mankato Collingwood London

Contents

Look for Tiger on the pages of this book. Sometimes he is hiding.

Tools are objects that people use to get a job done.

Fire hose

Hand Tools

We use most tools with our hands.

Some tools are very simple.

We learn to use
different tools.

What tools do you
know how to use?

spoon

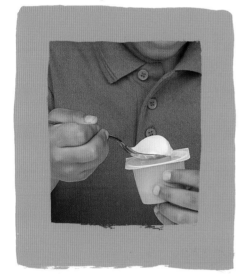

paintbrush

pan and brush

dishwashing brush

Twist and Turn

Twist a
pencil in a
sharpener.

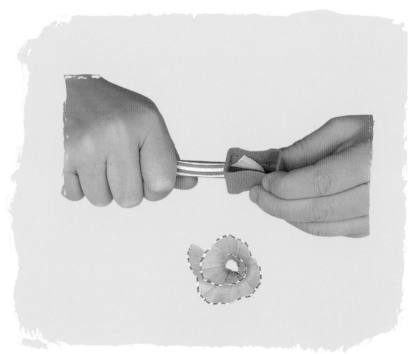

Turn a
paintbrush
in water.

Open
and
close
scissors.

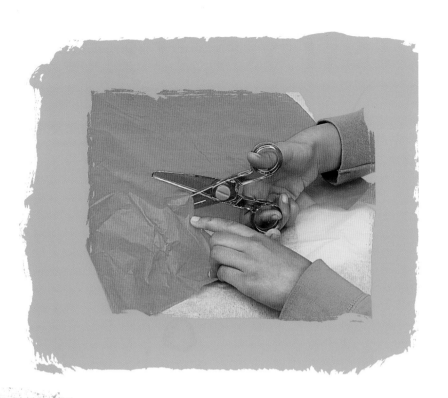

How do you
use a clay
cutter?

7

Terrific Tools

Tools have different uses.
Tools are used to...

cut things...

fix things...

hit things.

What can you do with a ruler?

?

In the Wrong Hands

Some tools are dangerous.

They can only be used by adults.

Some tools are:

sharp...

Don't play with dangerous tools.

Shears

hot...

Iron

or
heavy.

Hammer

Tools for the Job

People need tools to do their jobs.
Look at these tools.

A doctor's tools

Where would you find all these tools?

Fire hose

Police equipment

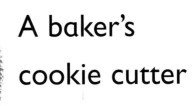
A baker's cookie cutter

Toy Tools

Toy tools
are fun to
play with.

I'm fixing
this door.

Helping Hand

We use tools to move things.

A wheelbarrow can carry a heavy load.

A shopping cart can carry heavy groceries.

What other tools help us move things around?

In the Yard

We use tools in
the yard.

We push and pull
a broom.

We push and
pull a trowel.

Look at these tools.
Which is the odd
one out?

19

Kitchen Tools

Maria is using tools to help her mom.

peeling vegetables

grating cheese

mashing potatoes

rolling out dough

whisking eggs

squeezing fruit

21

Tool List

We use lots of tools every day.

Carl has made a list of all the tools he used in one day.

The list reads (written upside down on the paper):

Tool list
a spoon
a hairbrush
a toothbrush
a pencil
scissors
an eraser
pencil sharpener

Tool list

a spoon

a hairbrush

a toothbrush

a pencil

scissors

an eraser

a pencil sharpener

Word Picture Bank

Fixing—page 14

Grating—page 20

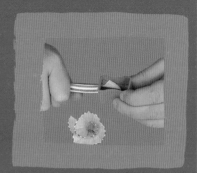

Pencil sharpener—page 6

Scissors—page 7

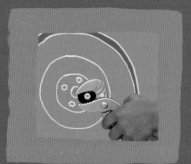

Wrench—page 15

Squeezing—page 21

This edition first published in 2011 by
Sea-to-Sea Publications
Distributed by Black Rabbit Books
P.O. Box 3263, Mankato, Minnesota 56002
Copyright © Sea-to-Sea Publications 2011
Printed in China, Dongguan

Library of Congress Cataloging-in-Publication Data
Read, Leon.
 Using tools / by Leon Read.
   p. cm. -- (Tiger talk: Get into science)
 Summary: "Provides young readers with an introduction to using basic
tools, and describes how these tools are used in their daily lives"--Provided
by publisher.
 ISBN 978-1-59771-253-8 (library bound)
 1. Tools--Juvenile literature. I. Title.
 TJ1195.R387 2011
 621.9--dc22
                              2009053792

9 8 7 6 5 4 3 2

Published by arrangement with the Watts Publishing Group Ltd, London.

Series editor: Adrian Cole
Photographer: Andy Crawford (unless otherwise credited)
Design: Sphere Design Associates
Art director: Jonathan Hair
Consultants: Prue Goodwin and Karina Law

Acknowledgments:
The Publisher would like to thank Norrie Carr model agency. Tiger Talk logo drawn
by Kevin Hopgood. Picture Credits: Corbis (17). Jochen Tach/Alamy (3).
Shutterstock (11b).

Every attempt has been made to clear copyright.
Should there be any inadvertent omission
please apply to the publisher for rectification.

March 2010
RD/6000006414/002

There are 17 Tigers, including me, in this book. Did you find all of us?